Clever Comprehension | Book 2

Contents   Page

DOWNLOAD FREE WORKSHEETS

&

EDUCATIONAL RESOURCES

Visit http://www.thetutoress.com/resources

for access.

Paper 1

Once on a Time

I am going to tell a story, one of those tales of astonishing adventures that happened years and years and years ago. Perhaps you wonder why it is that so many stories are told of "once on a time", and so few of these days in which we live; but that is easily explained.

In the old days, when the world was young, there were no automobiles nor flying-machines to make one wonder; nor were there railway trains, nor telephones, nor mechanical inventions of any sort to keep people keyed up to a high pitch of excitement. Men and women lived simply and quietly. They were Nature's children, and breathed fresh air into their lungs instead of smoke and coal gas; and tramped through green meadows and deep forests instead of riding in streetcars; and went to bed when it grew dark and rose with the sun--which is vastly different from the present custom. Having no books to read they told their adventures to one another and to their little ones; and the stories were handed down from generation to generation and reverently believed.

Those who peopled the world in the old days, having nothing but their hands to depend on, were to a certain extent helpless, and so the fairies were sorry for them and ministered to their wants patiently and frankly, often showing themselves to those they befriended.

So people knew fairies in those days, my dear, and loved them, together with all the Ryls and Knooks* and pixies and nymphs and other beings that belong to the hordes of immortals. A fairy tale was a thing to be wondered at and spoken of in awed whispers; for no one thought of doubting its truth.

Today fairies are shy; for so many curious inventions of men have come into use that the wonders of Fairyland are somewhat tame beside them, and even the boys and girls can not be so easily interested or surprised like they were in the old days. So the sweet and gentle little immortals perform their tasks unseen and unknown, and live mostly in their own beautiful realms, where they are almost unthought-of of by our busy, bustling world.

Yet when it comes to story-telling, the marvels of our own age shrink into insignificance beside the brave deeds and absorbing experiences of the days when fairies were better known; and so we go back to "once on a time" for the tales that we most love--and that children have ever loved since mankind knew that fairies exist.

*Ryls are immortal creatures. They watch over flowers and plants and are cousins to the Wood Nymphs.

*Knooks are also immortal creatures. They take care of the trees in the forest. They are big-hearted, kind and hard working.

An extract from *The Enchanted Island of Yew* by L. Frank Baum.

Answer the following questions.

Paragraph 2

1 The author says that people in the old days "went to bed when [4 m] it grew dark and rose with the sun." Why do you think this happened? Give evidence from the extract to support your answer.

They had nothing to do - they had no electricity so they couldn't see at night. 'nor were there railway trains or telephones...'

(3)

2 State a difference between people who lived in the old days [4 m] and the people who live today.

You may use the following structure to help you.

(a) The people who lived in the old days .... However, the people who live today .....

(b) Instead of .... like the people who lived in the old days, the people who live today ......

The people who lived in the old days had no books to read so instead reading they told their own stories however the people who live today have mountains of books to read.

(4)

Paragraph 3

3 Study this part of the extract: "Those who <u>peopled</u> the world in the old days, having nothing but their hands to depend on, were to a certain extent helpless……". [1 m]

Write another word for "peopled".   *Took over = populated*

Populated. (1)

4 Who did the fairies show themselves to? [1 m]

Underline the right answer. (1)

- Everyone who read books
- <u>Everyone they made friends with</u>
- Every boy and girl who looks for them

Paragraph 5

5 Why did the author describe the fairies as being "sweet and gentle"? Give evidence from the extract to support your answer. [3 m]

The author described them: ' patiently and frankly'; 'today fairies are shy'. (3)

6 An antonym is a word that is the opposite meaning of another. [5 m]

E.g. old – young

Write an antonym for each of the following words.

(a) children : adults ✓

(b) high : low ✓

(c) dark : light ✓

(d) quiet : loud ✓

(e) tame : wild ✓

⑤

7 A reflexive pronoun is usually used when the object of a sentence is the   [5 m]
same as the subject.

E.g. *"…the fairies were sorry for them and ministered to their wants patiently and frankly, often showing* **themselves** *to those they befriended."*

Fill in the blanks with the correct reflexive pronoun.

(a) She accidentally cut ___herself___ ✓ when she was chopping up apples for the pie.

⑤

(b) My son likes to dress ___himself___ in my husband's clothes.

(c) As soon as the cat came back indoors, it went to the fireplace to warm ___itself___ ✓.

(d) We were not proud to admit it, but we helped ___ourselves___ ✓ to the drinks and food at the launch party.

(e) I didn't believe in the existence of this creature until I saw it ___myself___ ✓

8 An adverb is used to modify verbs.   [5 m]

E.g. *"…the fairies were sorry for them and ministered to their wants* **patiently** *and* **frankly**…*"

Fill in the blanks with adverbs.

(a) The dog barked ___loudly___ at the approaching stranger. (*loud*) ✓

⑤

(b) James injured himself during the match last week and could ___hardly___ walk. (*hard*) ✓

(c) It was the last lesson of the last day of the semester and the students sat _restlessly_ in their seats. (*restless*) ✓

(d) He wrapped the autographed jersey _carefully_ ✓ in a piece of tissue and put it in his wardrobe. (*careful*)

(e) She spoke _dramatically_ ✓ about her appearance on the television show. (*dramatic*)

9   We use the words **some** and **any** for countable and uncountable nouns.   [5 m]
In general, we could say that **some** means *a few / a little* and **any** means *none* in negative clauses or *a few / a little* in sentences.

E.g.   *"…there were no automobiles nor flying-machines to make one wonder; nor were there railway trains, nor telephones, nor mechanical inventions of **any** sort to keep people keyed up to a high pitch of excitement."*

Fill in the blanks with *some* or *any*.

(a) I am going out to get _Some_ ✓ milk. Is there anything you need from the shop?

(b) This town is boring. I haven't seen _any_ ✓ spots I would like to explore.

(c) Tammy does not have _any_ ✓ pencils with her today. Would you lend her one of yours, please?

(d) William asked his mother for _Some_ ✓ money because there was a book he had to get for school.

(e) I am sure I made many mistakes in the test today. I should have studied _Some_ more last night! ✓

10   We use **indefinite pronouns** to refer to people or things without saying   [5 m]
exactly who or what they are.

For people we use: *anybody* or *anyone* | *somebody* or *someone* |
nobody or *no one* | *everybody* or *everything*
For things we use: *anything, something, nothing, none*

E.g. *"…Those who peopled the world in the old days, having **nothing** but their hands to depend on, were to a certain extent helpless…"*

Fill in the blanks with the correct indefinite pronouns. ✓

(a) My parents always told me that _anything_ is possible.

(b) After the festivities at the town hall, _everyone_ ✓ was invited to her house for an after-party. ✓

(c) James told _____nobody_____ about the bullying. We had absolutely no idea all these things were happening to him.

(d) Catherine was anxious on her first day because she did not see _____anyone_____ ✓ she knew in her new class.

(e) There is _____something_____ in the next room. What is it? ✓

Total Score: 37 /38

:) excellent

Rob's Workshop

"I tell you, Belinda, our son will be a great man one of these days," said Mr. Joslyn, walking up and down with pompous strides and almost bursting with the pride he took in his young hopeful.

Mrs. Joslyn sighed. She knew remonstrance was useless so long as her husband encouraged the boy, and that she would be wise to bear her cross with fortitude.

Rob also knew his mother's protests would be to no avail; so he continued to revel in electrical processes of all sorts, using the house as an experimental station to test the powers of his productions.

It was in his own room, however,--his "workshop"--that he especially delighted. For not only was it the centre of all his numerous "lines" throughout the house, but he had rigged up therein a wonderful array of devices for his own amusement. A trolley-car moved around a circular track and stopped regularly at all stations; an engine and train of cars moved jerkily up and down a steep grade and through a tunnel; a windmill was busily pumping water from the dishpan into the copper skillet; a sawmill was in full operation and a host of mechanical blacksmiths, scissors-grinders, carpenters, wood-choppers and millers were connected with a motor which kept them working away at their trades in awkward but persevering fashion.

The room was crossed and recrossed with wires. They crept up the walls, lined the floor, made a grille of the ceiling and would catch an unwary visitor under the chin or above the ankle just when he least expected it. Yet visitors were forbidden in so crowded a room, and even his father declined to go farther than the doorway. As for Rob, he thought he knew all about the wires, and what each one was for; but they puzzled even him, at times, and he was often perplexed to know how to utilize them all.

One day when he had locked himself in to avoid interruption while he planned the electrical illumination of a gorgeous pasteboard palace, he really became confused over the network of wires. He had a "switchboard," to be sure, where he could make and break connections as he chose; but the wires had somehow become mixed, and he could not tell what combinations to use to throw the power on to his miniature electric lights.

So he experimented in a rather haphazard fashion, connecting this and that wire blindly and by guesswork, in the hope that he would strike the right combination. Then he thought the combination might be right and there was a lack of power; so he added other lines of wire to his connections, and still others, until he had employed almost every wire in the room.

Yet it would not work; and after pausing a moment to try to think what was wrong he went at it again, putting this and that line into connection, adding another here and another there, until suddenly, as he made a last change, a quick flash of light almost blinded him, and the switch-board crackled ominously, as if struggling to carry a powerful current.

Rob covered his face at the flash, but finding himself unhurt he took away his hands and with blinking eyes attempted to look at a wonderful radiance which seemed to fill the room, making it many times brighter than the brightest day.

Although at first completely dazzled, he peered before him until he discovered that the light was concentrated near one spot, from which all the glorious rays seemed to scintillate.

He closed his eyes a moment to rest them; then re-opening them and shading them somewhat with his hands, he made out the form of a curious Being standing with majesty and composure in the centre of the magnificent radiance and looking down upon him!

The Demon of Electricity

Rob was a courageous boy, but a thrill of fear passed over him in spite of his bravest endeavour as he gazed upon the wondrous apparition that confronted him. For several moments he sat as if turned to stone, so motionless was he; but his eyes were nevertheless fastened upon the Being and devouring every detail of his appearance.

And how strange an appearance he presented!

His jacket was a wavering mass of white light, edged with braid of red flames that shot little tongues in all directions.

An extract from *The Master Key* by L Frank Baum.

Answer these questions.

Take a look at paragraphs 1 and 2

1   Mr. and Mrs. Joslyn had different attitudes towards Rob's experiments.   [2 m]
    How do their attitudes differ?

    You may use the following structure for your answer.

    Mr. Joslyn believed that …… Mrs. Joslyn, however, thought otherwise.
    She ……

    _____

    _____

    _____

Take a look at paragraph 4

2   Study the following sentence.   [2 m]

    *It was in his own room, however,--his "workshop"--that he especially
    delighted.*

    Why do you think the author used double inverted commas ("...") to
    describe Rob's workshop?

    _____

    _____

    _____

Re-read paragraph 5

3   Why do you think Mr. Joslyn "declined to go farther than the doorway" of   [4 m]
    Rob's room? Support your answer with evidence from the source.

    _____

    _____

_____

_____

_____

Read paragraph 10

4   Study the following sentence.   [1 m]

*Although at first completely dazzled, he peered before him until he discovered that the light was **concentrated** near one spot, from which all the glorious rays seemed to scintillate.*

Write another word for "concentrated".

_____

_____

5   After reading the extract, do you think Rob was an organized child who   [4 m]
knew what he was doing with his experiments? Support your answer
with evidence from the source.

_____

_____

_____

_____

_____

6   Collective nouns are used to refer to a group or collection of individuals,   [5 m]
    animals or things.

    E.g. – an array of devices

    Fill in the blanks with the correct collective noun.

        (a) a/an _____ of employees

        (b) a/an _____ of stars

        (c) a/an _____ of musicians

        (d) a/an _____ of hounds

        (e) a/an _____ of owls

7   Prepositions are placed before a noun (or a pronoun) to show the noun's   [5 m]
    (or the pronoun's) relationship to another word in the sentence.

    E.g. *A trolley-car moved **around** a circular track and stopped regularly at
    all stations; an engine and train of cars moved jerkily **up** and **down** a
    steep grade and **through** a tunnel; a windmill was busily pumping water
    from the dishpan **into** the copper skillet…"*

    Underline the correct preposition in each of the following sentences.

    (a) The mother and daughter are sitting (on, in, at) the kitchen table,
    having cups of tea.

    (b) Manchester lies about 40 metres (at, above, on) sea level.

    (c) The hills are covered with wildflowers (in, on, at) early spring.

    (d) They met at the restaurant (in, at, on) 6.00 p.m. and stayed (at, on,
    until) 10.00 p.m.

8   Prefixes are placed at the beginning of a word to change its meaning.   [5 m]

    E.g. *"They crept up the walls, lined the floor, made a grille of the ceiling
    and would catch an **unwary** visitor under the chin or above the ankle just
    when he least expected it."*

    Add the correct prefixes to the sentences below. Remember to use the correct tense.

il -	un -	im -	mis -	dis -

(a) It is ____ polite to interrupt when another person is speaking. Please wait until he has finished before you speak.

(b) Andrew could hardly contain his excitement. It was his birthday and he could not wait to ____ wrap the presents he had received.

(c) David stared at his test paper in ____ belief. He did not think he would do so well.

(d) I need to step out for a moment. Please do not ____ behave while I am not in the room.

(e) I have had enough of working with him on this project. His solutions to the problem are ____ logical.

9   Some words copy the sound of the action or object they are describing.   [5 m]
     This technique is known as onomatopoeia.

E.g. *"...as he made a last change, a quick flash of light almost blinded him, and the switch-board **crackled** ominously, as if struggling to carry a powerful current."*

Match the items on your left to the correct onomatopoeic word on the right.

(a)   Bees   •   •   (i)   gobble

(b)   Rivers   •   •   (ii)   fizzle

(c)   Telephones •   •   (iii)   gurgle

(d)   Sodas   •   •   (iv)   buzz

(e)   Turkeys   •   •   (v)   ring

10   We use superlatives to compare people and things. They are used to   [5 m]
      show that something or someone has a quality to the greatest or highest
      degree.

      E.g. *"…he took away his hands and with blinking eyes attempted to look
      at a wonderful radiance which seemed to fill the room, making it many
      times brighter than the* **brightest** *day…"*

      Fill in the blanks with the correct superlatives.

      (a) My brother is the _____ person in my family. (*tall*)

      (b) Nelly must be the _____ person I know! She has just
      won a trip to Europe in a contest! (*lucky*)

      (c) Pete is the _____ student in the class. (*funny*)

      (d) My grandmother bought the _____ cake in the shop for
      my sister's birthday party. (*big*)

      (e) Mrs. Pearson is the _____ teacher in school. All her
      students love her. (*good*)

Total Score: ____ /38

Paper 3

One bright morning as the Fox was following his sharp nose through the wood in search of a bite to eat, he saw a Crow on the limb of a tree overhead. This was by no means the first Crow the Fox had ever seen. What caught his attention this time and made him stop for a second look, was that the lucky Crow held a bit of cheese in her beak.

"No need to search any farther," thought sly Master Fox. "Here is a dainty bite for my breakfast."

Up he trotted to the foot of the tree in which the Crow was sitting, and looking up admiringly, he cried, "Good-morning, beautiful creature!"

The Crow, her head cocked on one side, watched the Fox suspiciously. But she kept her beak tightly closed on the cheese and did not return his greeting.

"What a charming creature she is!" said the Fox. "How her feathers shine! What a beautiful form and what splendid wings! Such a wonderful Bird should have a very lovely voice, since everything else about her is so perfect. Could she sing just one song, I know I should hail her Queen of Birds."

Listening to these flattering words, the Crow forgot all her suspicion, and also her breakfast. She wanted very much to be called Queen of Birds.

So she opened her beak wide to utter her loudest caw, and down fell the cheese straight into the Fox's open mouth.

"Thank you," said Master Fox sweetly, as he walked off. "Though it is cracked, you have a voice sure enough. But where are your wits?"

From 'The Fox & The Crow' by Aesop.

Answer these questions.

Look at paragraph 1

1   What was the Fox doing when he saw the Crow?   [2 m]

_____

_____

2   What does the author mean when he says that the Fox had a "sharp   [1 m]
    nose"?

_____

_____

Read paragraph 7

3   Why did the Crow open her beak wide to "utter her loudest caw"?   [4 m]
    Explain your answer.

_____

_____

_____

_____

_____

4   What was the Fox's strategy for getting the piece of cheese from the   [2 m]
    Crow's mouth?

_____

_____

5   The author of this story, Aesop, wrote a series of such stories, featuring   [4 m]
    animals, plants and inanimate objects. Collectively, these stories are
    known as "Aesop's Fables". Why did Aesop write such stories? Explain

your answer.

_____

_____

_____

_____

_____

6   Adjectives are words that describe or clarify nouns.   [5 m]

E.g. *Up he trotted to the foot of the tree in which the Crow was sitting, and looking up admiringly, he cried, "Good-morning, **beautiful** creature!"*

Underline the most appropriate adjectives in the following sentences.

(a) My mother makes (noisy, floppy, tasty) lasagne.

(b) Aunt Jane bought a (dainty, friendly, beautiful) cake for Mandy's birthday party. It was decorated with lots of sugar roses and leaves.

(c) My grandmother always wears a (noisy, floppy, tasty) hat when she goes to the beach to protect herself from the sun.

(d) The weather is (chilly, charming, salty). Please bring a cardigan.

(e) They moved out of their cramped apartment three years ago and now have a (dainty, furry, comfortable) home in the suburbs.

7   Action verbs are used to tell us what action someone or something is   [5 m]
     performing.

E.g. *The Crow, her head **cocked** on one side, **watched** the Fox suspiciously.*

Underline the most appropriate action verbs in the following sentences.

(a) He couldn't get to the ping-pong ball in time and it (told, bounced, sang) off the table onto the floor.

(b) After examining Sandra, the doctor (watched, worn, wrote) her a prescription and sent her to the nearest chemist's.

(c) As soon as she knew her favourite singer was having a concert in town, she went on-line and (bought, stuck, copied) a ticket for the performance.

(d) The stars (burned, twinkled, fell) brightly against the dark sky.

(e) The carpenter (torn, yelled, pounded) nails into the board.

8   We use inverted commas to mark the beginning and end of what someone says.   [5 m]

E.g. *"What a charming creature she is!" said the Fox.*

Insert inverted commas for the following sentences.

(a) Let's each lunch, said Denise, I'm hungry.

(b) Wow! These pictures are terrific! exclaimed Terry.

(c) I can't wait to go to school and tell the teacher about the things I learned, James said.

(d) The car, sighed Dad, needs to be taken to the mechanic.

(e) Perhaps you wouldn't be so tired, suggested Mum, if you went to bed earlier.

9   We use past progressive tense to describe continuing action that is happened in the past.   [5 m]

E.g. *One bright morning as the Fox was **following** his sharp nose through the wood in search of a bite to eat, he saw a Crow on the limb of a tree overhead.*

Fill in the blanks with the correct past progressive tense.

(a) Mr. Smith _____ the last two pieces of steak when his guest arrived. (*grill*)

(b) They _____ television all night long. (*watch*)

(c) John hardly had a break last weekend. He _____ his house. (*paint*)

(d) While the cat _____, the mice _____ the food. (*sleep, eat*)

10   We use nouns to define people, places and things in sentences. Proper nouns name specific people, places, things, or ideas, and they begin   [5 m]

with a capital letter.

Common nouns name people, places, things or ideas that are not specific. They do not start with a capital letter unless they begin a sentence.

E.g. *So she opened her **beak** wide to utter her loudest **caw**, and down fell the **cheese** straight into the **Fox**'s open **mouth**.*

Underline the nouns in the following sentences. There may be more than one in a sentence.

(a) Gerald is afraid of large dogs.

(b) The new couch looks amazing in the room.

(c) The students tried listening to the boring speech, but they fell asleep.

(d) While on a walk, Jeremy found a lost wallet on the ground.

(e) The little girl played with her friends in front of her house.

Total Score: _____ /38

1 "You are old, Father William," the young man said, "And your hair has become very white;

And yet you incessantly stand on your head – Do you think, at your age, it is right?"

5 "In my youth," Father William replied to his son, "I feared it might injure the brain;

But, now that I'm perfectly sure I have none,

Why, I do it again and again."

"You are old," said the youth, "as I mentioned before, And have grown most
10 uncommonly fat;

Yet you turned a back-somersault in at the door – Pray, what is the reason of that?"

"In my youth," said the sage, as he shook his grey locks, "I kept all my limbs very supple. By the use of this ointment – one shilling the box – Allow me to sell you a couple?"
15

"You are old," said the youth, "and your jaws are too weak For anything tougher than suet*;

Yet you finished the goose, with the bones and the beak – Pray how did you manage to do it?"

20 "In my youth," said his father, "I took to the law, And argued each case with my wife;

And the muscular strength, which it gave to my jaw, Has lasted the rest of my life."

"You are old," said the youth, "one would hardly suppose That your eye was as
25 steady as ever; Yet you balanced an eel on the end of your nose – What made you so awfully clever?"

"I have answered three questions, and that is enough," Said his father; "don't give yourself airs* Do you think I can listen all day to such stuff? Be off, or I'll kick you down stairs!"

*Suet means the fat around the organs of an animal.

*To give oneself airs means to be arrogant or stuck-up.

From the poem, 'You Are Old Father William' by Lewis Carroll.

Answer these questions.

1   Why did Father William stand incessantly on his head?   [2 m]

_____

_____

_____

2   How did Father William keep his limbs supple in his youth?   [1 m]

_____

_____

3   How did Father William develop muscular strength in his jaw?   [2 m]

_____

_____

_____

4   What are the young man's attitudes towards Father William's behaviour?   [4 m]
Support your answer with evidence from the source.

_____

_____

_____

_____

5   What are your opinions about Father William's behaviour at his age?   [4 m]
Explain your answer.

_____

_____

_____

_____

_____

6   We use question marks at the end of sentences to show that they are   [5 m]
     questions.

     E.g. Do you think, at your age, it is right?

     E.g. Pray, what is the reason of that?

     Direct questions are the "normal" questions that we can ask to friends,
     family members, and people whom we know well.

     Indirect questions are a little more formal and polite. We use them when
     talking to a person we don't know very well, or in professional situations,
     and their form is a little different. Some phrases for indirect questions
     include:

     - Could you tell me…
     - Do you know…
     - I was wondering…
     - Do you have any idea…
     - I'd like to know…
     - Would it be possible…
     - Is there any chance…

     Rewrite the following direct questions as indirect questions. Do not
     repeat the phrases you use.

     (a)   Where is the nearest mall?

     _____

     (b)   What's his name?

     _____

     (c)   When does the next train arrive?

     _____

     (d)   What time does the restaurant close?

     _____

(e)   Does Paul know anything about computers?

_____

7   We use conjunctions to join words, or groups of words together. Some   [5 m]
examples of conjunctions include: *and, or, but, nor, for, so,* and *yet.*

Fill in the blanks with the most appropriate conjunctions.

(a) Lily _____ her sister are going shopping this afternoon.

(b) Jason works really hard in school, _____ he does not do very well on his tests.

(c) We have to be there early, _____ we should leave the house now.

(d) Daniel does not like red, _____ does he like blue.

(e) Candice has a great family, a great job and lots of great friends, _____ she is a very unhappy person.

8   In punctuation, we use a dash (—) to show a pause or break in   [5 m]
meaning in the middle of a sentence, or an afterthought. Do not confuse
a dash with a hyphen. A hyphen (-) is used to join words to show that
their meaning is linked in some way.

E.g. *And yet you incessantly stand on your head – Do you think, at your age, it is right?*

Add dashes to the following sentences where appropriate.

(a) Timmy thought he knew the book very well until he saw the examination paper.

(b) Serena sang the song horribly and she thought she gave a brilliant performance.

(c) The teacher was saying, "Take out your books and" when the door flew open.

(d) We will invite Jessica she is the new girl next door to our party. (*add two dashes where appropriate*)

9   Contractions are shortened version of two words.   [5 m]

E.g. *Be off, or **I'll** kick you down stairs! (I will)*

Rewrite the sentences below, using contractions where necessary.

(a)   I will be home for the Christmas holidays.

_____

(b)   There is no milk in the refrigerator!

_____

(c)   It is hot and sunny today.

_____

(d)   George was not home last night.

_____

(e)   The store will not be open next Sunday.

_____

10   We use exclamation marks to express powerful feelings and to   [5 m]
emphasize important points.

E.g. *Be off, or I'll kick you down stairs!*

Question mark (?), full stop (.), or exclamation mark (!)? - Complete the following sentences with the most suitable punctuation mark.

(a) We won the match_____

(b) Are you ready for the test tomorrow_____

(c) What a moving performance_____

(d) I am shocked by what he has done_____

(e) Stay near the fire where it is warm_____

Total Score: /38

A colt, for blood and mettled speed,
The choicest of the running breed,
Of youthful strength and beauty vain,
Refused subjection to the rein.
In vain the groom's officious skill
Opposed his pride, and checked his will;
In vain the master's forming care
Restrained with threats, or soothed with prayer:
Of freedom proud, and scorning man,
Wild o'er the spacious plain he ran.
Where'er luxuriant Nature spread
Her flowery carpet o'er the mead,
Or bubbling stream's soft gliding pass
To cool and freshen up the grass,
Disdaining bounds, he cropped the blade,
And wantoned in the spoil he made.

In plenty thus the summer passed;
Revolving winter came at last:
The trees no more a shelter yield;
The verdure withers from the field:
Perpetual snows invest the ground;
In icy chains the streams are bound:
Cold, nipping winds, and rattling hail,
His lank, unsheltered sides assail.

As round he cast his rueful eyes,
He saw the thatched-roof cottage rise:
The prospect touched his heart with cheer,
And promised kind deliverance near.
A stable, erst his scorn and hate,
Was now become his wished retreat;
His passion cool, his pride forgot,
A Farmer's welcome yard he sought.

The master saw his woful plight,
His limbs, that tottered with his weight,
And, friendly, to the stable led,
And saw him littered, dressed, and fed.
In slothful ease all night he lay;
The servants rose at break of day;
The market calls. Along the road
His back must bear the pond'rous load;

In vain he struggles or complains,
Incessant blows reward his pains.
To-morrow varies but his toil:
Chained to the plough, he breaks the soil;
While scanty meals at night repay
The painful labours of the day.
Subdued by toil, with anguish rent,
His self-upbraidings found a vent.
"Wretch that I am!" he sighing said,
"By arrogance and folly led;
Had but my restive youth been brought
To learn the lesson nature taught,
Then had I, like my sires of yore,
The prize from every courser bore.
Now, lasting servitude's my lot,
My birth contemned, my speed forgot;
Doomed am I, for my pride, to bear
A living death from year to year."

From 'The Colt & The Farmer' by Harrison Weir.

Answer these questions.

Look at stanza 1

1   Why did the colt run away from his groom and master? Explain your   [2 m]
     answer.

     _____

     _____

     _____

Look at stanza 3

2   What did the colt do to escape from the cold of winter?   [1 m]

     _____

     _____

Read stanza 4

3   How did the farmer treat the colt initially? Explain your answer.   [2 m]

     _____

     _____

     _____

Look at stanza 5

4   How did the farmer treat the colt from the next day onwards? Explain   [4 m]
     your answer.

     _____

     _____

     _____

     _____

5   Did the colt regret running away from his first master? Why did he feel   [4 m]
    that way? Support your answer with evidence from the source.

    _____

    _____

    _____

    _____

    _____

6   Match the words on the left to their meanings on the right.   [5 m]

    (a) wanton   •   • (i)   meagre

    (b) verdure   •   • (ii)   regarded
                                             with disdain

    (c) erst   •   • (iii) unrestraint

    (d) scanty   •   • (iv)   formerly

    (e) contemned   •   • (v)   vegetation

7   A hyphen is used to join two or more words into a new word. This new   [5 m]
    word would have a combined meaning of the words that are joined
    together by the hyphen.

    E.g. *He saw the thatched-roof cottage rise…*

    E.g. *His self-upbraidings found a vent.*

    Insert hyphens in the following sentences where appropriate.

    (a) Keina is proud of her Japanese American heritage.

(b) Theresa's brother is a well-known journalist.

(c) The exquisite chandelier is an elegant addition to your dining room.

(d) The two year old boy fell off his bicycle and brawled in pain.

(e) Frank's father in law is retired and lives in Florida.

8   A suffix is a group of letters added to the end of a word to change its   [5 m]
    meaning.

E.g.   *The choicest of the running breed,*
       *Of **youthful** strength and beauty vain,*

Add the correct suffixes to the root words to complete the sentences
below.

- ful	- less	- able	- ible	- ous

(a) Are you absolutely sure these wild mushrooms are _____?
(*eat*)

(b) Serene did not think the lipstick she wore would be _____ —
until the head mistress asked her to wipe it all off. (*notice*)

(c) It is _____ to use the mobile phone while driving. (*danger*)

(d) We have been reminded to be _____ when we cross the road.
(*care*)

(e) Sometimes on a bad day, Sandra hates being a nurse; she feels that
it is a _____ job and nobody appreciates what she does. (*thank*)

9 Semicolons (;) are sometimes used instead of a full stop or period. This [5 m] is to separate sentences that are grammatically independent but that have closely connected meaning. Semicolons are also used for making lists clearer and for controlling the flow of text from one sentence to the next.

E.g. *In slothful ease all night he lay;*
The servants rose at break of day;
The market calls. Along the road

Insert semicolons where most appropriate in the following sentences.

(a) We watched the new film about penguins we didn't like it.

(b) Carmen wants to go into town Andrew wants to stay at home.

(c) The band members were: Kenny Daniels, vocals Ian Tanner, lead guitar Nathan Ormond, drums and Jake Rogers, bass guitar.

(d) Many people dislike stepping in the puddles and getting their shoes wet personally I find it fun and step into puddles with gusto.

(e) Debra had planned to visit her mother last week however, a problem developed at work and she couldn't get away.

10 A conjunction is a word that joins one part of a sentence to another. [5 m]

E.g. *Cold, nipping winds, **and** rattling hail,*
His lank, unsheltered sides assail.

Choose the best conjunction from the list below to join the following sentences together. Do not use each conjunction more than once.

but	since	because	so	when

(a) Laura gave her colleague a lift. It was raining heavily.

_____

(b) Jasmine would love to have a cat. Her mum didn't let her.

_____

(c) They were having pizza. We saw them at lunch.

_____

(d) Richard has been much happier. He made many friends at his new school.

_____

(e) Kim couldn't remember how to spell that word. She looked it up in the dictionary.

_____

Total Score: ___ /38

Answer Guide

Paper 1

1   The author says that people in the old days "went to bed when it grew   [4 m]
dark and rose with the sun". Why do you think this happened? Give
evidence from the extract to support your answer.

This could have happened because…

- there was no electricity to power appliances such as telephones.
There were also no mechanical inventions of any sort to keep
people keyed up to a high pitch of excitement. Without electric
lights or modern forms of entertainment like watching television
or playing games on the computer, the people in the old days
could not stay up late. Hence went to bed early and woke up
early too.

2   State 2 differences between people who lived in the old days and the   [4 m]
people who live today.

(a) The people who lived in the old days breathe fresh air
into their lungs. However, the people who live today
breathe smoke and coal gas.

(b) Instead of going to bed when it was dark and rising with
the sun like the people in the old days, the people who
live today probably go to bed very late and rise in the
middle of the day.

(c) The people who lived in the old days lived simply and
quietly. However, the people today are keyed up to a
high pitch of excitement due to the availability of
various mechanical inventions.

3   Look at this part of the extract: "Those who peopled the world in the old   [1 m]
days, having nothing but their hands to depend on, were to a certain
extent helpless……" Write another word for "peopled".

The word is…

- inhabited

- populated

4   To whom did the fairies show themselves?   [1 m]

Underline the right answer.

(everyone who reads books, **everyone they made friends with**, every child who searches for them)

5   Why did the author describe the fairies as "sweet and gentle immortals"? Give evidence from the extract to support your answer.   [3 m]

The author described the as the fairies as "sweet and gentle immortals" because…

- he thinks that fairies are sweet for being very helpful. For example, those who peopled the world in the old days were quite helpless, and so the fairies were sorry for them and ministered to their wants. As the fairies were kind-hearted and helpful, the author described them as "sweet".

- The fairies are patient with the people, very shy and show themselves to only those they befriended. Hence the author feels that they are very gentle and mild-tempered creatures.

6   An antonym is a word that is the opposite meaning of another.   [5m]

E.g. old – young

Write an antonym for each of the following words.

   (a)   children   :   **parents / adults**

   (b)   high   :   **low**

   (c)   dark   :   **light / bright**

   (d)   quiet   :   **noisy**

   (e)   tame   :   **wild**

7   A reflexive pronoun is usually used when the object of a sentence is the same as the subject.   [5m]

E.g. "…the fairies were sorry for them and ministered to their wants patiently and frankly, often showing **themselves** to those they befriended."

Fill in the blanks with the correct reflexive pronoun.

(a) She accidentally cut **herself** when she was chopping up apples for the pie.

(b) My son likes to dress **himself** in my husband's clothes.

(c) As soon as the cat came back indoors, it went to the fireplace to warm **itself**.

(d) We were not proud to admit it, but we helped **ourselves** to the drinks and food at the launch party.

(e) I didn't believe in the existence of this creature until I saw it <u>myself</u>.

8   (a) The dog barked **loudly** at the approaching stranger. (loud)   [5m]

(b) James injured himself during the match last week and could **hardly** walk. (hard)

(c) It was the last lesson of the last day of the semester and the students sat **restlessly** in their seats. (restless)

(d) He wrapped the autographed jersey **carefully** in a piece of tissue and put it in his wardrobe. (careful)

(e) She spoke **dramatically** about her appearance on the television show. (dramatic)

9   We use the words *some* and *any* for countable and uncountable nouns.   [5m]
In general, we could say that *some* means *a few / a little* and *any* means *none* in negative clauses or *a few / a little* in sentences.

E.g. "…there were no automobiles nor flying-machines to make one wonder; nor were there railway trains, nor telephones, nor mechanical inventions of **any** sort to keep people keyed up to a high pitch of excitement."

Fill in the blanks with *some* or *any*.

(a) I am going out to get **some** milk. Is there anything you need from the shop?

(b) This town is boring. I haven't seen **any** spots I would like to explore.

(c) Tammy does not have **any** pencils with her today. Would you lend her one of yours, please?

(d) William asked his mother for **some** money because there was a book he had to get for school.

(e) I am sure I made many mistakes in the test today. I should have studied **some** more last night!

10   We use indefinite pronouns to refer to people or things without saying   [5m]
exactly who or what they are.

For people we use: anybody or anyone | somebody or someone |
nobody or no one | everybody or everyone
For things we use: anything, something, nothing, none

E.g. "…Those who peopled the world in the old days, having **nothing** but their hands to depend on, were to a certain extent helpless…"

Fill in the blanks with the correct indirect pronouns.

(a) My parents always told me that <u>anything</u> is possible.

(b) After the festivities at the town hall, <u>everyone</u> was invited to her house for an after-party.

(c) James told <u>nobody</u> about the bullying. We had absolutely no idea all these things were happening to him.

(d) Catherine was anxious on her first day because she did not see <u>anyone</u> she knew in her new class.

(e) There is <u>something</u> in the next room. What is it?

Answer Guide

Paper 2

1   Mr. and Mrs. Joslyn had different attitudes towards Rob's experiments.   [2 m]
    How do their attitudes differ?

    You may use the following structure for your answer.

    Mr. Joslyn believed that …… Mrs. Joslyn, however, thought otherwise.
    She ……

    - Mr. Joslyn believed that Rob was going to be a successful man with
      great achievements. Mrs. Joslyn, however, thought otherwise. She
      was doubtful of Rob's capabilities and did not think he would
      succeed in his efforts

2   Study the following sentence.   [2 m]

    *It was in his own room, however,--his "workshop"--that he especially
    delighted.*

    Why do you think the author used double inverted commas ("...") to
    describe Rob's room?

    - The author is trying to imply / suggest that Rob thinks of the room
      as his workshop when it is actually just his bedroom.

3   Why do you think Mr. Joslyn "declined to go farther than the doorway"   [4 m]
    of Rob's room? Support your answer with evidence from the source.

    - Mr. Roslyn probably declined to go farther than the doorway of
      Rob's room because it was crowded with his devices and wires
      were crossed and recrossed. Mr. Roslyn probably thought the room
      was dangerous and hence did not want to enter the room.

4   Study the following sentence.   [1 m]

    *Although at first completely dazzled, he peered before him until he
    discovered that the light was concentrated near one spot, from which
    all the glorious rays seemed to scintillate.*

    Write another word to for "concentrated".

The word is

- focused

- directed

5   After reading the extract, do you think Rob was an organized child who   [4 m]
     knew what he was doing with his experiments? Support your answer
     with evidence from the source.

     I do not think Rob was an organized child who knew what he was doing
     because:

- Rob "workshop" was crossed and recrossed with his many wires
  and devices and it was so disorganized that visitors to the room
  tripped on, or got caught in the wires.

- Rob was experimenting in a rather haphazard fashion,
  connecting wires blindly and by guesswork, in the hope that he
  would strike the right combination. This suggests that he was
  not working in an organized manner at all and did not know what
  he was doing.

6   Collective nouns are used for a group or collection of individuals,   [5m]
     animals or things.

     E.g. – an array of devices

     Fill in the blanks with the correct collective noun.

          (a) a/an **staff** of employees

          (b) a/an **galaxy** of stars

          (c) a/an **band** of musicians

          (d) a/an **pack** of hounds

          (e) a/an **parliament** of owls

7   Prepositions are placed before a noun (or a pronoun) to show the   [5m]
     noun's (or the pronoun's) relationship to another word in the sentence.

     E.g. A trolley-car moved **around** a circular track and stopped regularly
     at all stations; an engine and train of cars moved jerkily **up** and **down** a
     steep grade and **through** a tunnel; a windmill was busily pumping
     water **from** the dishpan **into** the copper skillet…"

Underline the correct preposition in each of the following sentences

(a) The mother and daughter are sitting (on, in, **at**) the kitchen table, having cups of tea.

(b) Manchester lies about 40 metres (at, **above**, on) sea level.

(c) The hills are covered with wildflowers (**in**, on, at) early spring.

(d) They met at the restaurant (in, **at**, on) 6.00 p.m. and stayed (at, on, **until**) 10.00 p.m.

8   Prefixes are placed at the beginning of a word to modify or change its meaning.   [5m]

E.g. "They crept up the walls, lined the floor, made a grille of the ceiling and would catch an **unwary** visitor under the chin or above the ankle just when he least expected it."

Add the correct prefixes to the sentences below.

il -	un -	im -	mis -	dis -

(a) It is **im**polite to interrupt when another person is speaking. Please wait until he has finished before you speak.

(b) Andrew could hardly contain his excitement. It was his birthday and he could not wait to **un**wrap the presents he had received.

(c) David stared at his test paper in **dis**belief. He did not think he would do so well.

(d) I need to step out for a moment. Please do not **mis**behave while I am not in the room.

(e) I have had enough of working with him on this project. His solutions to the problem are **il**logical.

9   Some words imitate the sound of the action or object they are describing. This technique is known as onomatopoeia.   [5m]

E.g. "...as he made a last change, a quick flash of light almost blinded him, and the switch-board **crackled** ominously, as if struggling to carry a powerful current."

Match the items on your left to the correct onomatopoeic word on the right.

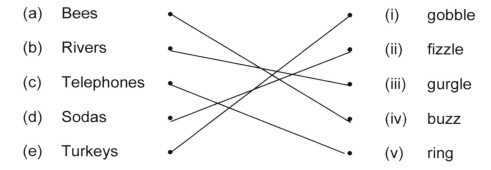

(a)	Bees	(i)	gobble
(b)	Rivers	(ii)	fizzle
(c)	Telephones	(iii)	gurgle
(d)	Sodas	(iv)	buzz
(e)	Turkeys	(v)	ring

10   We use superlatives to compare people and things. They are used to show that something or someone has a quality to the greatest degree.   [5m]

E.g. "…he took away his hands and with blinking eyes attempted to look at a wonderful radiance which seemed to fill the room, making it many times brighter than the **brightest** day…"

Fill in the blanks with the correct superlatives.

(a) My brother is the **tallest** person in my family. (*tall*)

(b) Nelly must be the **luckiest** person I know! She has just won a trip to Europe in a contest! (*lucky*)

(c) Pete is the **funniest** student in the class. (*funny*)

(d) My grandmother bought the **biggest** cake in the shop for my sister's birthday party. (*big*)

(e) Mrs. Pearson is the **best** teacher in school. All her students love her. (*good*)

Answer Guide

Paper 3

1   What was the Fox doing when he saw the Crow?   [2 m]

  - The Fox was following his sharp nose and looking for something to eat when he met the Crow.

2   What does the author mean when he says that the Fox had a "sharp   [1 m]
    nose"?

  - The means that the Fox had a very keen sense of smell.

3   Why did the Crow open her beak wide to "utter her loudest caw"?   [4 m]
    Explain your answer with evidence from the source.

  - The Crow opened her beak wide to "utter her loudest caw" because the Fox had been piling praises at her and wondered if the crow could sing just one song so that he could hail her Queen of Birds. The Crow badly wanted to be called the Queen of Birds and hence she wanted to the Fox to hear her voice. Hence she opened her beak wide to utter he loudest caw.

4   What was the Fox's strategy for getting the piece of cheese from the   [2 m]
    Crow's mouth?

  - The Fox's strategy for getting the Crow's cheese was to use the praises to break down the suspicions of the Crow and to get the Crow to acknowledge, or respond to his praises. When the Crow opens her mouth to acknowledge and respond to his praises, the cheese will fall straight into the Crow's mouth.

5   The author of this story, Aesop, wrote a series of such stories, featuring   [4 m]
    animals, plants and inanimate objects. Collectively, these stories are known as "Aesop's Fables". Why did Aesop write such stories? Explain your answer.

  - Aesop wrote such stories to highlight a moral lesson. Aesop was trying to remind people to be cautious towards flatterers. Just like the Crow who fell for the flattery of the Fox and lost her cheese, readers of the story should not fall for flattery or they might lose something too.

6   Adjectives are words that describe or clarify nouns.   [5m]

E.g. *Up he trotted to the foot of the tree in which the Crow was sitting, and looking up admiringly, he cried, "Good-morning, **beautiful** creature!"*

Underline the most appropriate adjectives in the following sentences.

(a) My mother makes (noisy, floppy, **tasty**) lasagne.

(b) Aunt Jane bought a (dainty, friendly, **beautiful**) cake for Mandy's birthday party. It was decorated with lots of sugar roses and leaves.

(c) My grandmother always wears a (noisy, **floppy**, tasty) hat when she goes to the beach to protect herself from the sun.

(d) The weather is (**chilly**, charming, salty). Please bring a cardigan.

(e) They moved out of their cramped apartment three years ago and now have a (dainty, furry, **comfortable**) home in the suburbs.

7   a) bounced   [5m]
     b) wrote
     c) bought
     d) twinkled
     e) pounded

8   We use inverted commas to mark the beginning and end of what   [5m]
     someone says.

E.g. "What a charming creature she is!" said the Fox.

Insert inverted commas for the following sentences.

(a) "Let's each lunch," said Denise, "I'm hungry."

(b) "Wow! These pictures are terrific!" exclaimed Terry.

(c) "I can't wait to go to school and tell the teacher about the things I learned," James said.

(d) "The car," sighed Dad, "needs to be taken to the mechanic."

(e) "Perhaps you wouldn't be so tired," suggested Mum, "if you went to bed earlier."

9   a) was grilling   [5m]
     b) were watching
     c) was painting

d) was sleeping, were eating

10   We use nouns to define people, places and things in sentences. Proper   [5m]
     nouns name specific people, places, things, or ideas and they begin
     with a capital letter.

     Common nouns name people, places, things or ideas that are not
     specific. They do not start with a capital letter unless they begin a
     sentence.

     E.g. So she opened her **beak** wide to utter her loudest **caw**, and down
     fell the **cheese** straight into the **Fox**'s open **mouth**.

     Underline the nouns in the following sentences. There may be more
     than one in a sentence.

     (a) **Gerald** is afraid of large **dogs**.

     (b) The new **couch** looks amazing in the **room**.

     (c) The **students** tried listening to the boring **speech**, but they fell
     asleep.

     (d) While on a **walk**, **Jeremy** found a lost **wallet** on the **ground**.

     (e) The little **girl** played with her **friends** in front of her **house**.

Answer Guide

Paper 4

1   Why did Father William stand incessantly on his head?   [2 m]

  - When Father William was young, he wanted to stand on his head but did not do that because he thought it would injure his brain. When he got older, he felt it was not going to be a problem because he felt sure that he did not have any brain to injure anyway.

2   How did Father William keep his limbs supple in his youth?   [1 m]

  - In his youth, he kept his limbs supple by using a box of ointment.

3   How did Father William develop muscular strength in his jaw?   [2 m]

  - He developed muscular strength in his jaw by arguing each case with his wife. They must have argued very frequently because all the arguing strengthened his jaw muscles.

4   What are the young man's attitudes towards Father William's behaviour?   [4 m]
    Support your answer with evidence from the source.

  - The young man seemed to disapprove of Father William's behaviour. He asked Father William if it was right for Father William, at his age, to stand incessantly on his head. This shows that the young man did not really approve of Father William's behaviour. He also thought that Father William was too fat to be able to do a back-somersault, too weak to be able to finish a whole goose and too old to have a steady gaze. These suggests that the young man did not seem to think very highly of Father William's capabilities, assuming that Father William was too old, too weak and too fat to be able to do what he did.

5   What are your opinions about Father William's behaviour at his age?   [4 m]
    Explain your answer.

  - I do not think it is wrong or inappropriate for Father William to be doing all these things at his age. I actually think it is commendable that Father William was not restricted by his age and continued doing things like standing incessantly on his head and turning a back-somersault. Father William also seemed to have a sense of humour. This is apparent when he said that it was alright for him to stand on his head because he did not have any brain to injure, and also when he implied that he developed strong jaw muscles through constant arguments with his wife.

6   We use question marks at the end of sentences to indicate questions.   [5 m]

E.g.   Do you think, at your age, it is right?

E.g. Pray, what is the reason of that?

Direct questions are the "normal" questions that we can ask to friends, family members, and people whom we know well.

Indirect questions are a little more formal and polite. We use them when talking to a person we don't know very well, or in professional situations, and their form is a little different. Some phrases for indirect questions include:

- Could you tell me…
- Do you know…
- I was wondering…
- Do you have any idea…
- I'd like to know…
- Would it be possible…
- Is there any chance…

Rewrite the following direct questions as indirect questions. Do not repeat the phrases you use.

(a) **Could you tell me** where the nearest mall **is**?

(b) **Do you have any idea** what his name **is**?

(c) **I'd like to know** when the next train **arrives**.

(d) **Would it be possible to know** what time the restaurant **closes**?

(e) **I was wondering if** Paul knows anything about computers.

7   We use conjunctions to join words, or groups of words together. Some   [5 m]
examples of conjunctions include: *and, or,* but, *nor, for, so,* and *yet*.

Fill in the blanks with the most appropriate conjunctions. Use commas when necessary.

(a) Lily **and** her sister are going shopping this afternoon.

(b) Jason works really hard in school, **but** he does not do very well on his tests.

(c) We have to be there early, **so** we should leave the house now.

(d) Daniel does not like red, **nor** does he like blue.

(e) Candice has a great family, a great job and lots of great friends, **yet** she is a very unhappy person.

8   In punctuation, we use a dash (—) to show a pause or break in meaning in the middle of a sentence, or an afterthought. Do not confuse a dash with a hyphen. A hyphen (-) is used to join words to show that their meaning is linked in some way.   [5 m]

E.g. *And yet you incessantly stand on your head – Do you think, at your age, it is right?*

Add dashes to the following sentences where appropriate.

(a) Timmy thought he knew the book very well — until he saw the examination paper.

(b) Serena sang the song horribly — and she thought she gave a brilliant performance.

(c) The teacher was saying, "Take out your books and — " when the door flew open.

(d) We will invite Jessica — she is the new girl next door — to our party. (*add two dashes where appropriate*)

9   Contractions are shortened version of two words.   [5 m]

E.g. Be off, or I'll kick you down stairs! (I will)

Rewrite the sentences below, using contractions where necessary.

(a) **I'll** be home for the Christmas holidays.

(b) **There's** no milk in the refrigerator!

(c) **It's** hot and sunny today.

(d) George **wasn't** home last night.

(e) The store **won't** be open next Sunday.

10   We use exclamation marks to express powerful feelings and to   [5 m]
      emphasize important points.

      E.g. *Be off, or I'll kick you down stairs!*

      Question mark (?), full stop (.), or exclamation mark (!)? - Complete the
      following sentences with the most suitable punctuation mark.

      (a) We won the match.

      (b) Are you ready for the test tomorrow?

      (c) What a moving performance!

      (d) I am shocked by what he has done!

      (e) Stay near the fire where it is warm.

Answer Guide

Paper 5

1   Why did the colt run away from his groom and master? Explain your answer.   [2 m]

- The colt ran away because he was young, strong and stubborn. He hated the control of his groom and master and hence ran away to be free.

2   What did the colt do to escape from the cold of winter?   [1 m]

- The colt sought refuge at a farmer's yard to escape from the cold of winter.

3   How did the farmer treat the colt initially? Explain your answer.   [2 m]

- Initially the farmer treated the colt very well and with kindness. The colt was housed in the stable where he had fresh litter and food. The farmer also dressed the colt's wound and allowed him to rest in the stable.

4   How did the farmer treat the colt from the next day onwards? Explain your answer.   [4 m]

- From the next day onwards, the farmer treated the colt cruelly. The farmer's servant made the colt carry a heavy a heavy load. The colt was beaten if he struggled and he was also made to plough the fields. Yet for all his hard work, the colt received little to eat.

5   Did the colt regret running away from his first master? Why did he feel that way? Support your answer with evidence from the source.   [4 m]

- The colt regretted running away from his first master. He sighed at his fate and called himself a "wretch". He admitted that he had been restless, proud and foolish in his youth, to have run away from his first master. He felt that if he had remained with his first master, he would have at least been able to run and race the way he was born for. However, he was a trapped slave with the farmer, unable to realize his true potential.

6   Match the words on the left to their meanings on the right.   [5 m]

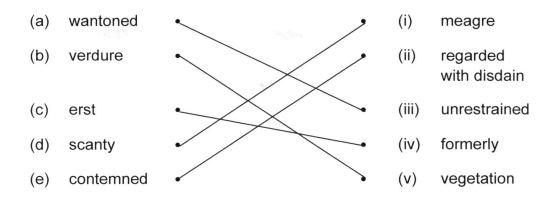

(a) wantoned   (i)   meagre

(b) verdure   (ii) regarded
                                                       with disdain

(c) erst   (iii) unrestrained

(d) scanty   (iv) formerly

(e) contemned   (v)   vegetation

7   A hyphen is used to join two or more words into a new word. This new   [5 m]
     word would have a combined meaning of the words that are joined
     together by the hyphen.

     E.g. *He saw the thatched-roof cottage rise…*

     E.g. *His self-upbraidings found a vent.*

     Insert hyphens in the following sentences where appropriate.

     (a) Keina is proud of her **Japanese-American** heritage.

     (b) Theresa's brother is a **well-known** journalist.

     (c) The exquisite chandelier is an elegant addition to your **dining-room**.

     (d) The **two-year-old** boy fell off his bicycle and brawled in pain.

     (e) Frank's **father-in-law** is retired and lives in Florida.

8   A suffix is a group of letters added to the end of a word to change its   [5 m]
     meaning.

     E.g. *The choicest of the running breed,*
           *Of **youthful** strength and beauty vain,*

     Add the correct suffixes to the root words to complete the sentences below.

- ful	- less	- able	- ible	- ous

(a) Are you absolutely sure these wild mushrooms are **edible**? (*eat*)

(b) Serene did not think the lipstick she wore would be **noticeable** — until the head mistress asked her to wipe it all off. (*notice*)

(c) It is **dangerous** to use the mobile phone while driving. (*danger*)

(d) We have been reminded to be **careful** when we cross the road. (*care*)

(e) Sometimes on a bad day, Sandra hates being a nurse as she feels that it is a **thankless** job and nobody appreciates what she does. (*thank*)

9   Semicolons (;) are sometimes used instead of a full stop or period. This is to separate sentences that are grammatically independent but that have closely connected meaning. Semicolons are also used for making lists clearer and for controlling the flow of text from one sentence to the next.   [5 m]

E.g. *In slothful ease all night he lay;*
The servants rose at break of day;
The market calls. Along the road

Insert semicolons where most appropriate in the following sentences.

(a) We watched the new film about penguins; we didn't like it.

(b) Carmen wants to go into town; Andrew wants to stay at home.

(c) The band members were: Kenny Daniels, vocals; Ian Tanner, lead guitar; Nathan Ormond, drums; and Jake Rogers, bass guitar.

(d) Many people dislike stepping in the puddles and getting their shoes wet; personally I find it fun and step into puddles with gusto.

(e) Debra had planned to visit her mother last week; however, a problem developed at work and she couldn't get away.

10   A conjunction is a word that joins one part of a sentence to another.   [5 m]

E.g. *Cold, nipping winds, **and** rattling hail,*

His lank, unsheltered sides assail.

Choose the best conjunction from the list below to join the following sentences together. Do not use each conjunction more than once.

but	since	because	so	when

(a)   Laura gave her colleague a lift. It was raining heavily.

Laura gave her colleague a lift **because** it was raining heavily.

(b)   Jasmine would love to have a cat. Her mum didn't let her.

Jasmine would love to have a cat **but** her mum didn't let her.

(c)   They were having pizza. We saw them at lunch.

They were having pizza **when** we saw them at lunch.

(d)   Richard has been much happier. He made many friends at his new school.

Richard has been much happier **since** he made many friends at his new school.

(e)   Kim couldn't remember how to spell that word. She looked it up in the dictionary.

Kim couldn't remember how to spell that word **so** she looked it up in the dictionary.

About The Author

Since 2010, The Tutoress (founded by Miss Olubi) and her team of dedicated tutors have helped hundreds of children to pass the 11+ school entrance exams. As a result of such committed efforts, The Tutoress has maintained an incredible success rate (97% in 2013) and has quickly risen to become one of the leading providers of 11+ tuition in the UK.

Miss Olubi and her team hold fun yet highly effective holiday classes, workshops and intensive courses for students who want to excel in the 11+ exams and beyond. For more information and for access to free education resources visit www.thetutoress.com/resources.

Further Resources by The Tutoress

Clever Comprehension: KS2 Reading & Comprehension Practice Book 1

Available on

Amazon.co.uk

Amazon USA

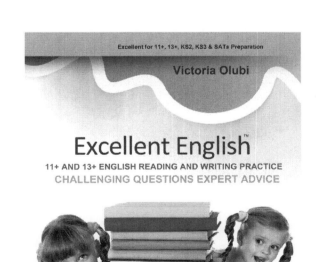

Excellent English: 11+ Reading & Writing Practice

Available on

Amazon.co.uk

Amazon.com

Printed in Germany
by Amazon Distribution
GmbH, Leipzig